TO LEARN MORE ABOUT NFI AND THE *DOCTOR DAD*® PROGRAMS:

TRAINING, TECHNICAL ASSISTANCE AND QUESTIONS ABOUT THE DOCTOR Dad® PROGRAMS

Phone: (301) 948-0599
Fax: (301) 948-4325
Email: programsupport@fatherhood.org
Website: www.fatherhood.org

LEARN MORE ABOUT NATIONAL FATHERHOOD INITIATIVE

20410 Observation Drive
Suite 107
Germantown, MD 20876

Phone: (301) 948-0599
Fax: (301) 948-4325
Email: info@fatherhood.org
Website: www.fatherhood.org

- blog.fatherhood.org
- www.facebook.com/nationalfatherhoodinitiative
- @thefatherfactor
- www.fatherhood.org/dademail

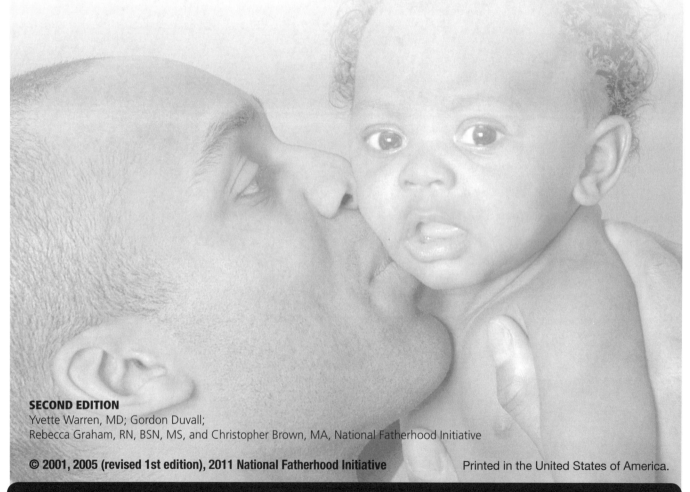

SECOND EDITION
Yvette Warren, MD; Gordon Duvall;
Rebecca Graham, RN, BSN, MS, and Christopher Brown, MA, National Fatherhood Initiative

© 2001, 2005 (revised 1st edition), 2011 National Fatherhood Initiative   Printed in the United States of America.

ATTENTION: Trademark and Copyright Protection
The manuals, inventories and other instructional materials published by the National Fatherhood Initiative are federally protected against unauthorized reproduction whether print or electronic.

Table of Contents

6 The Purpose of Doctor Dad®

9 The Safe Child

10 Car Safety

12 Kitchen Safety

14 Bathroom Safety

16 Bedroom Safety

18 Living Room Safety

20 Yard Safety

22 Gun Safety

25 Parental Anger

27 The Safe Child Learning Review

28 Appendix

29 Learning Review Answer Key

30 Important Phone Numbers, Addresses, and E-mails

31 Room Safety Checklists

34 Glossary of Medical Terms

THE SAFE CHILD
FATHER'S HANDBOOK

DOCTOR DAD® WORKSHOPS

The Purpose of Doctor Dad®

The purpose of Doctor Dad® is two-fold:

1. To increase fathers' parenting skills in the area of infant and toddler health.
2. To help fathers realize that they play a unique role in caring for their children.

Increasing Parenting Skills for Infant and Toddler Health:

Caring for your child's health and safety might not come as easily as we think. Dads don't get a manual when they bring their babies home from the hospital.

Your child's doctor will spend a lot of time in the first few months of your child's life teaching you about the basics of health and safety. You can partner with your child's doctor to make sure that your child has a healthy start by learning as many skills as possible during Doctor Dad®.

Did you know that you play a unique role in caring for your children whether you live with your child or not?

Dad's parenting style is different from moms' parenting style. Scientists know that children grow better and can be healthier if you use your unique style.

Did you know that when you are involved in your child's life that your child is more likely to get healthcare and less likely to be injured at home?

Different Parenting Style:

Name a few ways that your parenting style is different from mom's style:

_____

_____

_____

Dads' and Moms' parenting styles are different. One is not better than the other.

Did you know that being involved right from the start affects your child's health for a lifetime?

> **REMEMBER!** Your children need your unique parenting style. They will be healthier when you are involved.

Health and Healthcare of Children	When Dads Are Involved	When Dads Are Not Involved
Poverty	Children are less likely to be poor.	Children are 5 times more likely to be poor.
Healthcare Visits	Children are more likely to see their doctor for regular checkups or when they are sick.	Children are less likely to see their doctor for regular checkups or when they are sick.
Safety	Children have less chance of being in an accident, getting injured, or being poisoned.	Children have a 20-30% higher chance of having accidents, injuries, or poisonings.
Child Abuse	A father's involvement in the physical care of his child before age 3 reduces the chance that he will sexually abuse his child.	Father absence is one of the most common predictors of child abuse.
Neglect		Risk of neglect is doubled.

During Doctor Dad® Workshops: The Safe Child, you will learn about:

- Keeping your child safe in the:
    - ▶ home
    - ▶ car
    - ▶ backyard
- Sudden Infant Death Syndrome (SIDS)
- Gun safety
- The dangers of parental anger

These are just a few of the skills that you will learn in this workshop. You will learn the basics about health and safety. You will not learn how to be a doctor. It will be helpful to remember several things as you go through the session.

- **There are no silly questions.**
  Be sure to check with your child's doctor if you have any questions about your child's health.

- **Every child is different.**
  You will learn basic information in the workshop. If your child has special needs, always check with your child's doctor.

- **Call for help if you have a medical emergency.**

Medical Disclaimer

The information contained in this book has been prepared by licensed medical professionals; the material therefore conforms to accepted medical practices in most circumstances. However, such information and statements contained here are necessarily general in nature. As such, the information and statements may not be comprehensive nor are they intended to dictate the appropriate course of treatment in all situations. Care or action differing from that derived here may be required either because of differing community standards or because of observations and conclusions, which can only be made on a case-by-case basis.

Always consult your doctor or medical care provider before acting with respect to any individual case.

National Fatherhood Initiative, its officers, board members, and employees deny any and all liability for any injuries, losses, claims, damages, and expenses arising from or related to the information in this material. Acceptance and use of the information constitutes agreement to this disclaimer of liability.

The Safe Child

The information in this section covers **"the basics"** on creating a safe home and surroundings for your child. **Always** consult your child's doctor if you have questions about creating a safe home and surroundings. Remember that all children are different. You might need to create special ways to create a safe home if your child has special needs.

Car Safety

Identify safe and unsafe situations in the car.

Write the correct age ranges for each car seat underneath each picture.

Infant/Toddler

Age Range:

_____

_____

Toddler/Preschooler

Age Range:

_____

_____

What can I do to make my child safe in the car?

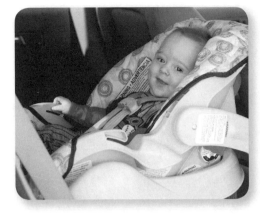

Make sure that you secure your child in the appropriate safety seat.

The Safe Child

> **REMEMBER!**
> All children 12 and younger should sit in the backseat.

	Infants/Toddlers	Toddlers/Preschoolers
Age, Height, and Weight	Birth to 24 months (2 years) old, and up to the highest weight and height allowed by the manufacturer of the car seat	Older than 24 months (2 years), and up to the highest height and weight allowed by the manufacturer of the car seat
Type of Seat	Rear-facing	Forward-facing
Seat Position	Rear-facing	Forward-facing
		Harness straps should be at or above shoulders.

Notes:

_____

_____

_____

_____

Kitchen Safety
Identify Safe and Unsafe Situations in the Kitchen

The Safe Child

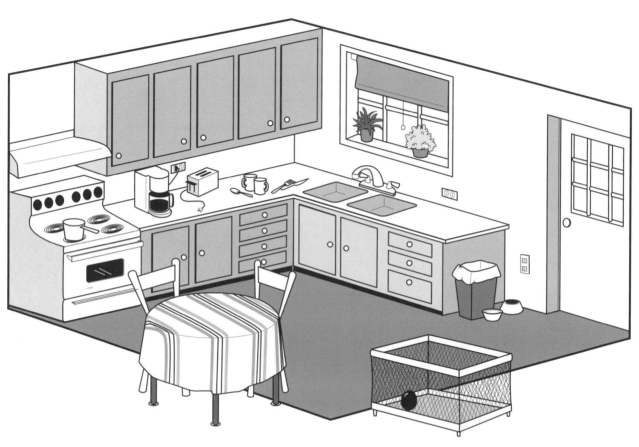

Notes:

Notes:

Bathroom Safety
Identify Safe and Unsafe Situations in the Bathroom

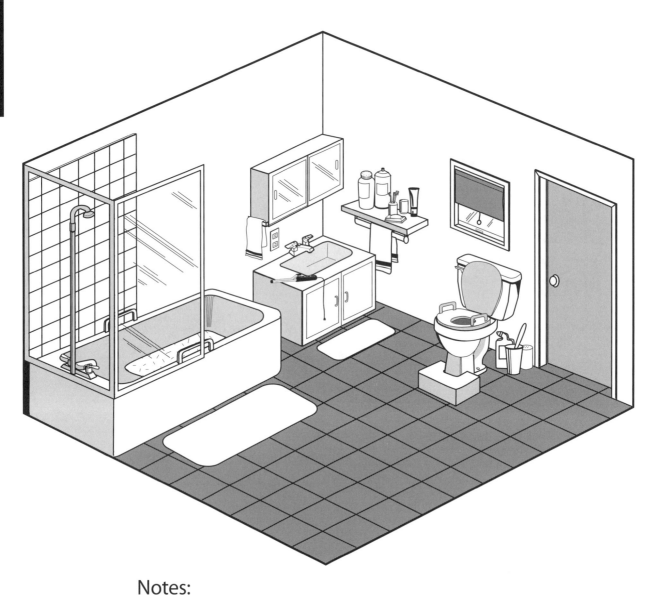

Notes:
_____
_____
_____
_____
_____
_____

Notes:

_____
_____
_____
_____
_____
_____
_____
_____
_____
_____
_____

Bedroom Safety
Identify Safe and Unsafe Situations in the Bedroom

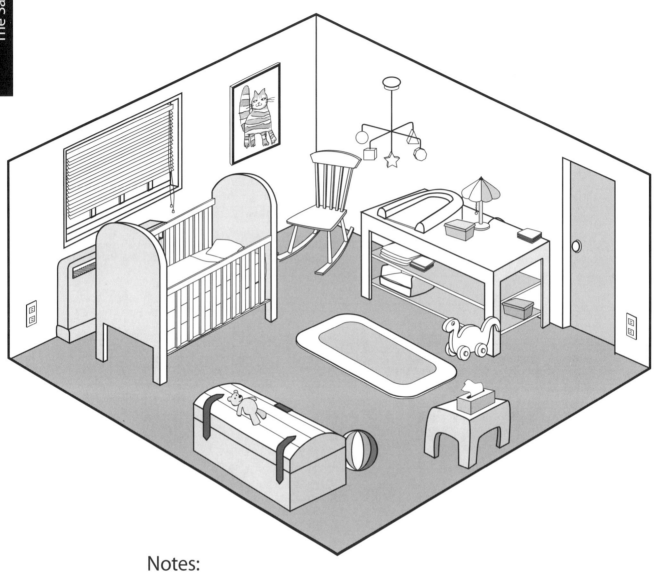

Notes:
___
___
___
___
___
___

SIDS

What is SIDS?
Sudden Infant Death Syndrome (SIDS) is the leading cause of death in babies between the first month and the end of the first year of life. Sadly, no one knows the cause of SIDS.

How can I prevent SIDS?
Gladly, we do know that fathers can reduce the risk of SIDS by:

- Placing babies on their backs to sleep.
- Having mothers not smoke while pregnant and no smoking by either parent in the home after the baby is born.
- Encouraging mothers to get prenatal care from the moment they know that they are pregnant.

What is the best position for my baby to sleep in?
The best position is on his or her back. In 1993 the American Academy of Pediatrics started their "Back to Sleep" campaign. They said that, to lower the risk of SIDS, all babies should be placed on their backs to sleep. The SIDS rate has been greatly reduced since the start of this campaign.

Suffocation
Suffocation isn't the same as SIDS. Suffocation occurs when the airway or face is blocked or covered. You can prevent suffocation in your children.

How can I lower the risk of my child suffocating?
- Don't let your child sleep on a waterbed.
- Don't place your child on beanbags chairs.
- Don't place pillows in your child's crib.
- Don't place your child on a couch to sleep.
- Don't sleep in the same bed with your child, especially if you or mom has been using alcohol or drugs.

What can I do to make a crib safe?
Make a few simple measurements. Crib rails should be at least 26 inches from the top of the mattress. Bars should be no more than 2 3/8 inches apart (the width of a soda can). The mattress should fit snuggly in the crib with no room for your child to get between the mattress and rails. Position the crib away from windows and radiators.

> **WARNING!**
> Babies might not start to roll over until age 4-6 months. If they are placed on a soft surface, they will not be able to turn over, which places them at higher risk for suffocation.

Living Room Safety
Identify Safe and Unsafe Situations in the Living Room

Notes:

_____
_____
_____
_____
_____
_____

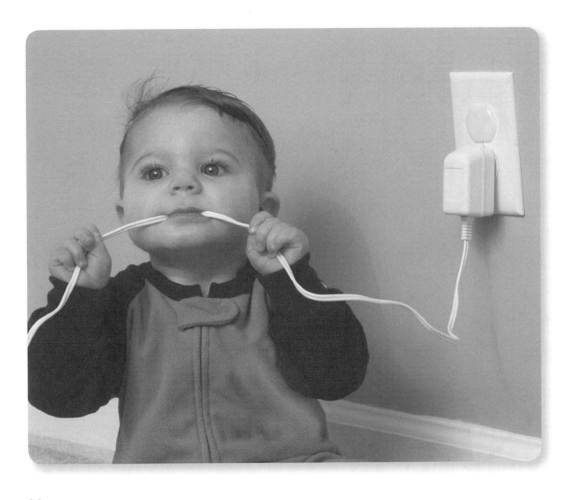

Notes:

Yard Safety
Identify Safe and Unsafe Situations in the Yard

Notes:

_____
_____
_____
_____
_____
_____

Notes:

The Safe Child

Gun Safety

What do dads need to know about gun safety?

According to the Centers for Disease Control and Prevention, injuries from firearms are the second-leading cause of non-natural death among children and teens in the U.S. No other country reports more accidental firearms deaths among children under the age of 15.

Most shooting deaths result from one or more children playing with a gun they find in the home. The person who pulls the trigger is a friend, family member, or the victim. Children who were involved in accidental gun injuries were more likely to be boys who were playing at home with friends and were not being watched by an adult.

> **WARNING!**
> Most shooting deaths result from one or more children playing with a gun they find in the home. The person who pulls the trigger is a friend, family member, or the victim.

What can I do to make my home "gun safe?"

The best way is to not have a gun in the home. If you decide to keep guns in your home:

- Keep them in a locked area, away from children.
- Keep safety trigger locks on them, even when stored in a locked area.
- Keep ammunition stored in a different place than a gun, also in a locked area.
- Never let your children know where the gun or ammunition is stored.

> Children who were involved in accidental gun injuries were more likely to be boys who were playing at home with friends and were not being watched by an adult.

National Fatherhood Initiative | www.fatherhood.org

Notes:
_____
_____
_____
_____
_____
_____
_____
_____
_____

Parental Anger

It's important to know that we all get angry at times. Anger is a normal emotion that all parents have. The key is to know how to handle anger and frustration when it occurs.

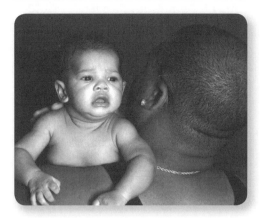

It's also helpful to know your child's style, (temperament) and to have realistic expectations about your child's behavior.

If you know, for example, that your child is "a difficult baby," and finds change hard, you will expect your child to cry and fuss when he or she is in a new or bad setting. You will also know why your child reacts the way that he or she does.

What can I do to make my child's world calmer?

1. Turn off TV's, radios, video games, or other sources of noise.
2. Play calming music.
3. Turn down the lights.
4. Speak in a soft whisper or hum a song for your child.

The Period of PURPLE Crying

Starting at about two weeks of age, some babies begin crying more often and might be hard to soothe. The crying can last for hours. If your child is not sick and you have tried everything you can think of to soothe the baby, it is okay if you can't stop your baby from crying. Don't feel guilty and don't get angry with your child. Not being able to soothe an infant does not make you a bad parent.

Some babies are just going to cry. It will end, and life will return to normal. The letters in PURPLE stand for the common parts of non-stop crying in infants:

- **P** - Peak pattern (crying peaks around 2 months, then lessens)
- **U** - Unpredictable (crying for long periods can come and go for no reason)
- **R** - Resistant to soothing (the baby may keep crying for long periods)
- **P** - Pain-like look on face
- **L** - Long bouts of crying (crying can go on for hours)
- **E** - Evening crying (baby cries more in the afternoon and evening)

 For more information on the Period of PURPLE Crying visit the Shaken Baby Syndrome website at **www.dontshake.org**.

REMEMBER! Never Shake Your Child!

Each year children die or get brain damage because a frustrated parent or caregiver shook them. It's important to know that all parents get frustrated. But it's <u>never</u> okay to take out frustration on your child.

Make a plan about how you will handle your anger if you think it's getting out of control.

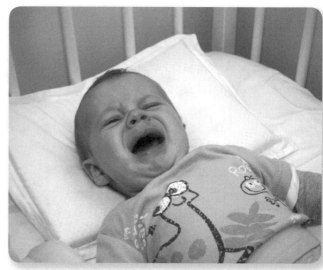

Some things you can do to handle your anger include:

- Call someone you can talk to or someone who can give you a break.

- Put your child in a safe place, like the crib or playpen, and go into another room for a short time and get yourself together.

- Promise yourself that you will never shake your baby. Shaking your baby can cause brain damage or death.

REMEMBER!

Children have fragile bodies and emotions.

So remember:
- **Don't yell at them.**
- **Don't shake them.**
- **Don't abuse them with harsh words.**
- **Children watch what you do, so you will teach your child to yell and hit if that is how you handle anger.**

The Safe Child Learning Review

Circle the correct answer.

1. I can keep my child safe in the car if he or she needs to sit in my lap. — True / False

2. As soon as my child turns 1 year old, I will be able to put my child in a forward-facing car seat. — True / False

3. I can help prevent burns in the kitchen by turning pot handles towards the back of the stove when cooking. — True / False

4. One of the best ways to keep the bathroom safe is to keep the door closed. — True / False

5. I can lower the risk of SIDS in my child by encouraging his or her mom not to smoke. — True / False

6. Placing my baby on his or her back when he or she sleeps is another way to lower the risk of SIDS. — True / False

7. All parents get angry and frustrated sometimes with their children, but I know that I should never shake my child. — True / False

8. Shaking my child when I am angry can cause brain damage or death in my child. — True / False

Answers can be found on page 29 in the Appendix.

Learning Review Answer Key

The Safe Child Learning Review Answers

1. False. You can never keep your child safe in the car while he or she sits in your lap. Each year thousands of children die because they are not properly restrained in a car seat.

2. False. Your child must be 1 year and weigh 20 lbs. to be safely moved to a forward-facing car seat. If your child turns 1 year of age and has not reached the 20 lb. mark, he or she must stay in a rear-facing infant seat.

3. True.

4. True.

5. True.

6. True.

7. True.

8. True.

Appendix

- Use a pen or pencil to record your child's most recent weight.

- Cut around dotted line and keep it near your phone.

- If you have more than one child, make copies of this page to have one for each child.

- Make some extra blank copies to complete as your child grows and if numbers and addresses change.

- Include this information in yours and mom's mobile phones if you have to get to it when out of the house or out of town.

Important Phone Numbers, Addresses, and E-mails

Today's Date: _____

Child's Name: _____
Date of Birth: _____
Most Recent Weight: _____
Allergies: _____
Most Recent Height: _____

Our Phone Number: _____
Our Address: _____
Our Email Address: _____

Child or Family Doctor: _____
Doctor Phone Number: _____
Doctor Address: _____
Doctor E-mail: _____

Friends and Family to Call in an Emergency: _____
_____

Child's Name: _____
Date of Birth: _____
Most Recent Weight: _____
Allergies: _____
Most Recent Height: _____

Our Phone Number: _____
Our Address: _____
Our Email Address: _____

Child or Family Doctor: _____
Doctor Phone Number: _____
Doctor Address: _____
Doctor E-mail: _____

Friends and Family to Call in an Emergency: _____
_____

POLICE: 911 or _____
FIRE: 911 or _____
POISON CONTROL: 1-800-222-1222

Room Safety Checklists

Nothing guarantees your child's safety like watching your child, but don't think that watching your child is enough. Think about what your baby is doing now, what he or she will be doing next, and where he or she might be doing it. You should get on the floor to get a "child-size" view on his or her world.

Kitchen

- ☐ Clear counter
- ☐ Appliances put away when not in use
- ☐ No loose cords
- ☐ Oven/stove locks
- ☐ Cabinets secured
- ☐ Handles of pots turned to rear of stove
- ☐ Remove tablecloth
- ☐ Trash secured and out of reach
- ☐ Pet food/water put away
- ☐ Knives & sharp items put away
- ☐ Cleaning supplies out of reach or locked
- ☐ Electric socket covers in place

> Never leave your child alone in your kitchen.

Bathroom

- ☐ Electric socket covers in place
- ☐ Electric appliances put away
- ☐ Cleaning supplies put away
- ☐ Toilet lid lock in place
- ☐ Shaving accessories put away
- ☐ Medications/cosmetics out of reach
- ☐ Non-slip tub mat
- ☐ Faucet cover/padding
- ☐ Hot water heater set below 120 degrees

> Never leave your child alone, and keep the bathroom door closed, if possible.

Bedroom

- ☐ Snug-fitting crib mattress
- ☐ No pillows or stuffed animals in crib
- ☐ Working smoke detector
- ☐ Electric socket covers in place
- ☐ Window blind cords tied up and out of reach
- ☐ Radiator/heater covered
- ☐ Safe toy box, no heavy lid
- ☐ Crib away from window
- ☐ Window secured, gated if above 1st floor
- ☐ All baby care supplies put away

Living room

- ☐ Working smoke detector
- ☐ Electric socket covers in place
- ☐ Bookcases secured to wall
- ☐ Knick-knacks put up out of reach
- ☐ Houseplants placed out of reach
- ☐ Electric cords taped down
- ☐ Curtain cords tied up and out of reach
- ☐ Door lock out of reach
- ☐ Table corners padded
- ☐ Gates at top and bottom of stairs
- ☐ Pictures/mirrors out of reach
- ☐ Electronic equipment out of reach

> Never put an infant to sleep on the couch or leave your child alone in the living room.

Garage

- ☐ Put tools up out of reach
- ☐ Lock/secure toolboxes
- ☐ Put chemicals away
- ☐ Unplug electric tools
- ☐ Secure all electric cords
- ☐ Working smoke detector
- ☐ Put away lawn mower and other lawn tools

> Never leave your child alone in the garage.

Outside of House

- ☐ Identify and eliminate poisonous plants
- ☐ Avoid strange pets & animals
- ☐ Clean up trash
- ☐ Put away pet food & water
- ☐ Lock gate
- ☐ Secure pool with locking gate
- ☐ Safety seats for swings
- ☐ Put away all tools

> Never leave your child alone outide your home.

Car

- ☐ Working seat belts
- ☐ Proper sized car seat
- ☐ Emergency kit
- ☐ First aid kit
- ☐ Cell phone
- ☐ Safe treaded tires
- ☐ Put dangerous items out of reach

> Never leave your child alone in the car, especially when it's hot outside.

Glossary of Medical Terms

This glossary defines helpful terms related to the health and wellness of your child. You might find some of these terms used in your handbook. There are other terms included that are not in the handbook, but are useful terms to know.

Adverse Reaction: A response to a medicine or treatment that is acting against or in the wrong way, unfavorable, not what was meant to happen.

Ambulatory Care: Medical care received outside of the hospital. For example, well child check-ups, routine physicals, etc.

Antibiotic: A medicine used to fight or kill a disease caused by bacteria. Antibiotics will not kill viruses.

Antibodies: Proteins that are the basis for the human immune system. Antibodies are proteins made by the body after exposure to an illness or vaccine. Antibodies are used by the body to fight infection.

Asthma: A disorder marked by difficulty in breathing, wheezing and coughing. Asthma is often caused by allergies.

Asymptomatic: No symptoms; being without a sign that reveals a disease or abnormality.

Autism: A mental disorder starting in infancy that is characterized esp. by an inability to interact socially, repetitive behaviors and language disorders.

Botulism: A disease caused by a bacteria often found in tainted foods.

Calories: The units for measuring heat; used on food labels to tell how much energy is found in a food.

Cognitive Development: The growth of one's mental skills, such as thinking, remembering, learning and language.

Congenital Rubella: German Measles existing at or dating from birth.

Diphtheria: A very bad infection that usually attacks the throat and nose. It is easily passed from one person to another and can kill someone. In more serious cases, it can attack the nerves and heart. Because of widespread immunization, diphtheria is very rare in the United States. Some people, however, don't get the shot to prevent diptheria, so cases still occur.

Electrolyte Imbalances: The loss of body fluids due to lots of vomiting, diarrhea, sweating or high fever can lead to imbalances of electrolytes. Electrolytes can carry an electrical charge. They are found in the blood, tissue fluid and cells of the body. Common electrolytes in the body include sodium, potassium, calcium and magnesium. Imbalances in any of these electrolytes can result in serious health problems.

Failure to Thrive: Failure to thrive describes children whose current weight or rate of weight gain is far below that of other children of similar age and sex.

Father Hunger: Sleep disturbances, such as trouble falling asleep, nightmares and night terrors often begin one to three months after father leaves the home. Often afflicts boys 1 to 2 years of age whose fathers leave suddenly.

Fever: A rise in body temperature above the normal, which is defined as a range, not a single number.

Forage: To search for food or supplies.

Hydrocortisone Cream: Steroid cream that decreases inflammation.

Hypoxia: To not have enough oxygen in blood/system.

Immune system: The system that protects the body from foreign substances, cells and tissues by producing the immune response, which fights off infections. This system includes the thymus, spleen, lymph nodes and lymphocytes.

Immunizations: Substances given to make a person immune to a particular illness. Can be given by mouth or injected, depending on type.

Infected: Being affected by a disease or condition caused by a germ or parasite.

Infectious Diseases: A condition caused by a germ or parasite causing an abnormal bodily condition that impairs functioning and can usually be recognized by signs and symptoms that present as a sickness.

Intracranial: Inside the skull; enclosing the brain.

Intravenous fluids: Fluids being given by way of the veins. Fluids may be administered for fluid replacement due to dehydration or for administration of medication/nutrients.

Malnutrition: Faulty and especially inadequate nutrition.

Mercurochrome: A solution of iodine used as a local antiseptic.

Misconception: The process of not conceiving or not being conceived. The inability to form or understand ideas or concepts.

Morbidity: The incidence of disease, the rate of sickness (as in a specified community or group).

Mortality: The number of deaths in a given time or place. The proportion of deaths to population, the death rate.

Nurturance: The promotion of growth and development of all of one's traits, qualities and characteristics.

Nutrition: The act or process of nourishing; especially the processes by which a person takes in and uses food.

Prone Positioning: Lying face down, on stomach.

Psychologist: A person trained to study the science of mind and behavior.

Pyloric Stenosis: A condition that affects the gastrointestinal tract during infancy; a narrowing of the outlet of the stomach. This condition can cause your baby to vomit forcefully; may cause other problems such as dehydration and salt and fluid imbalances.

Reactive Airways: (See Asthma)

Rhinorrhea: Nasal discharge, usually mucus; material that comes out of the nose.

Seizure: A sudden attack that affects the central nervous system causing an abnormal and violent involuntary contraction or series of contractions of muscle.

Septic Work-up: A procedure used to identify the cause of sepsis, which is an infection that affects the entire body. The work-up could include but is not limited to: blood & urine cultures, spinal tap and throat cultures.

Solid Foods: Nutrition for the body that is not liquid.

SPF: (Skin or sun protective factor) a rating scale for the strength of sunscreen.

Stature: The natural height of a person.

Suffocation: The act or result of being stifled, smothered or choked.

Tetanus: An infectious disease caused by bacterial poisons and marked by muscle stiffness and spasms especially of the jaws.

Trachea: The main tube by which air enters the lungs; windpipe.

Tympanic thermometer: Takes the temperature measurement from the eardrum.

Vaccines: A single or group of materials (as a preparation of killed or weakened virus or bacteria) used in vaccinating to induce immunity to a disease.

Virus: Any of a large group of submicroscopic infectious agents that can grow and multiply only in living cells, and that cause diseases.